CW01187519

HIBA NOOR KHAN Illustrated by SALINI PERERA

INSPIRING INVENTORS
WHO ARE CHANGING OUR FUTURE

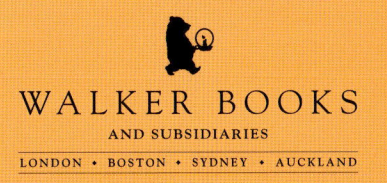

WALKER BOOKS
AND SUBSIDIARIES
LONDON · BOSTON · SYDNEY · AUCKLAND

CONTENTS

Mohammed Bah Abba 6-7

Ann Makosinski 8-9

Joshua Silver 10-11

René Favaloro 12-13

Marita Cheng 14-15

Kevin Kumala 16-17

Sarah Toumi 18-19

Reem Al Marzouqi 20-21

Sonam Wangchuk 22-23

Temple Grandin 24-25

Brian Gitta 26-27	Wilhelm Röntgen 36-37
Abeer Seikaly 28-29	Makoto Murase 38-39
Emma Camp 30-31	Topher White 40-41
Sara Saeed 32-33	Pearl Kendrick & Grace Eldering 42-43
Gloria Asare 34-35	Richard Turere 44-45

ABOUT THIS BOOK

Your mind and heart are as unique as the tiny grooves that form your fingerprint. No one else anywhere in the world thinks and feels in exactly the same way you do, and that is one of the things that makes human beings so incredible. We all have our very own way of looking at and experiencing the world around us, as well as our own individual set of skills and talents.

In this book, you'll explore the lives, inspirations and inventions of twenty-one amazing people. And they aren't just "any old" inventors… All of them have used their minds and hearts **together** in clever ways to come up with something new – tapping into their unique abilities and experiences to make the world we live in a better place, from the deserts of Tunisia to the coral reefs of Bali.

Look for the "Great Minds" panels, and there you'll meet inventors from across the ages who have also created something unique and important. Some of them are brilliant minds from history, who laid the foundations for the inspiring inventors in this book, while others have come up with different solutions to similar problems around the world.

These inventors might have been as young as you are now when they began inventing and designing … and lots of them have proved that you don't need to attend university, or be a maths super genius, to become an inventor. Many of the inventions you'll read about were thought up far, far away from a science lab – whether that's on a farm in the USA, in the Indonesian jungle, during rainstorms in Japan or in a rural Nigerian village.

But their inventors have one important thing in common: all of them saw or experienced a problem, and decided to work hard to help fix it.

Science, technology and engineering have given us all sorts of things that were once unimaginable. Think about trying to explain the internet to someone who lived three hundred years ago! Since ancient times, people have challenged their minds and come up with so many new ideas and tools. While lots of inventions have revolutionized the way we live in positive ways, they don't always make our world a better, fairer place… After all, destructive weapons were also invented by human minds.

The magic combination, to be an **ethical** inventor, is to use your heart and mind together. Your mind might be able to invent something super smart and sophisticated, but when you add heart, you and your designs become powerful in the best way. When we use our brains to figure out ways to help people in need, to care for animals, and to protect and revive our planet, we become change-makers and ground-breakers.

We all have the power to create and invent. You are making thoughts and building ideas even as you read these words! Just as many of our wonderful inventors were inspired by others who went before them, perhaps you too will find a spark of inspiration on these pages.

The world awaits what only YOUR unique mind and heart can bring to it.

MOHAMMED BAH ABBA (1964—2010)
THE ZEER POT IN NIGERIA

Mohammed Bah Abba was born in Nigeria, where extreme heat can make it difficult to keep food fresh. With no electricity for fridges, farmers in Mohammed's village were struggling; by market day, their fruit and vegetables had already wilted under the sun.

Mohammed had grown up watching his grandfather mould pots, carefully shaping clay before baking it on an open fire: a simple but skilful craft, and an ancient African tradition. These pots were already designed to keep water cold – so Mohammed began to experiment, fitting one pot inside another, then filling the gap with damp sand. He discovered that the inner pot became much colder, and remained so for much longer than before.

With this, the amazing "Zeer" pot was born! At once, farmers saw results: the Zeer pot kept tomatoes, peppers and aubergines fresh for three weeks or more. Delighted, Mohammed set up five pot factories in different villages, and paid for the first 5,000 Zeers himself. With these pots farmers can trade goods for a fair price, and their young daughters, who had been helping to sell their crops before they rotted, can stay in school.

ANCIENT AFRICAN SCIENCE
There is historical evidence that cooling techniques like Mohammed's were used in ancient Egypt, as early as 2500 BCE, but later largely forgotten by the world – especially once electric fridges came along.

HOW IT WORKS

1. One clay pot is fitted inside another; the gap is filled with moist sand.

2. Water from the sand evaporates through the outer clay pot, into the air.

3. As the water evaporates, it also carries heat away from the centre pot – cooling the food inside.

4. The sand only needs to be wetted twice a day to keep the Zeer pot working!

GOOD NEWS TRAVELS FAST!

Mohammed's invention spread across northern Nigeria, as well as Cameroon, Chad, Eritrea and Sudan. A new version of the Zeer pot is now also used to store important medicines.

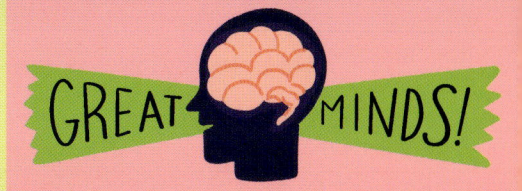

— DID YOU KNOW? —

Clay pots have been used for centuries across the world to cool food and drink, from the botijo in Spain to the matki in India and Pakistan.

GREAT MINDS!

Supermarkets and shops have to throw away lots of food reaching the end of its shelf-life, while many people go without because they can't afford to buy food. After heading to bed hungry for much of his childhood, OSCAR EKPONIMO created an app called Chowberry which tells shops when food is about to go out of date – allowing them to sell these items at a lower price, for people who can't afford full-price. This has helped millions of people in Nigeria, and also helps avoid food waste!

Each year many Uruguayan farmers' lemons, oranges and other fruits are ruined by icy weather, a problem that's getting worse due to climate change. Engineer RAFAEL GUARGA designed a fan that sucks up cold air before it has a chance to create frost, releasing it 100m above the trees where air is warmer – saving a lot of money, effort and fruit!

HOW IT WORKS

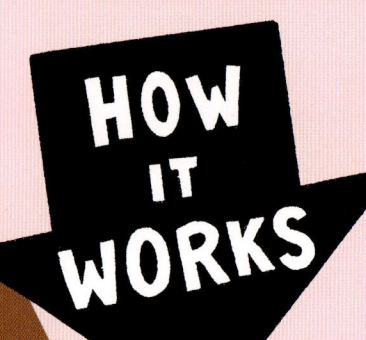

ANN MAKOSINSKI
THE HOLLOW FLASHLIGHT IN CANADA

1. The flashlight uses special tiles that produce electricity when one side is warm and the other is cool.

2. The tiles are placed around a hollow tube.

3. When the person's hand warms the outside, an aluminium tube cools the inside.

4. The resulting temperature difference provides electrical energy that lights the bulb at the end of the torch, without any batteries or solar power!

Instead of a teddy or doll, Ann's first toy was a box of electrical "transistors"! Her parents encouraged her to be creative, and growing up she loved taking things apart to see how they worked.

When she was just fifteen years old, Ann spoke to a friend living out in the Philippines (where Ann's mother had grown up); the friend was failing in school because her family couldn't afford electricity, and she desperately needed light in order to study at night.

Ann knew that, at any moment, the human body produced enough heat energy to power a lightbulb – which gave her an idea. Soon after, she had designed the amazing hollow flashlight: fairly cheap to make, and using only the heat of the human body, the flashlight has the potential to provide people with access to light, which many of us take for granted.

Ann is now fascinated with the untapped energy of the human body, and hopes that, in the future, she will be able to harness it in her work towards tackling climate change.

KEY PHRASE: RENEWABLE ENERGY

Renewable energy is made from things that nature will continuously replace, like water, sunlight and wind. These forms of energy production don't release carbon dioxide or pollute the earth like fossil fuels (gas, coal and oil) do.

–DID YOU KNOW?–

Wind was first harnessed by humans in ancient times to sail ships across the sea. The first practical wind power plants were constructed in Sīstān, in seventh-century Persia, to pump water and grind grains, and then in twelfth-century China.

FIRST WINDMILL

James Blyth created the first windmill to produce electricity in Glasgow in 1887, and one of his designs powered his home for 25 years!

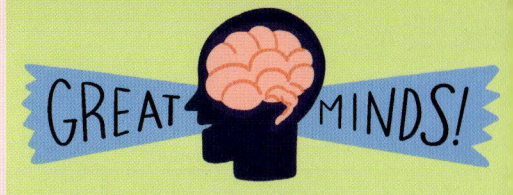

GREAT MINDS!

In 1839, ALEXANDRE-EDMOND BECQUEREL discovered that shining light can produce electricity. ALBERT EINSTEIN later developed this fascinating science into the basis for solar panels, which use light from the sun to produce electricity.

MÁRIA TELKES was nicknamed "The Sun Queen" because of her many solar-powered inventions. In the 1940s in America, Mária and her team designed and built the world's first fully solar-heated house. She also invented solar-powered ovens, ideal for villagers in sunny regions, and a solar-powered system for purifying water – making even seawater drinkable!

JOSHUA SILVER
THE SELF-ADJUSTING GLASSES IN THE UK

Joshua Silver has always been fascinated by how we see. When he wasn't working as a Physics professor, he would unwind by playing with lenses for a hobby!

He knew that, if someone had sight problems, a good pair of glasses could give them access to an education, work and safety, as well as the ability to see their loved ones and the world around them. But in most countries, to get a pair of glasses, you need to visit an optician who can test your eyes and prescribe the right lenses.

One day, while having tea with a friend, Joshua began to wonder about people living in poorer countries, without access to an optician – was there a way to help them? Could he design glasses that could be adjusted by the person wearing them, without an optician?

He returned home and began designing the same afternoon: within ten minutes, he had an ingenious plan for glasses that he produced, tested and wore himself, giving him clear vision!

DID YOU KNOW?
When the lens in your eye becomes clouded, sight is blurred, eventually leading to blindness. This is called a cataract, and is the cause of a third of the blindness in the world.

VISION!
Joshua's vision is to be able to give vision to the whole world.

HOW IT WORKS

GOOD NEWS TRAVELS FAST!
Joshua's glasses design has been distributed to thousands of people in more than 20 countries, improving quality of life everywhere from Pakistan to Ghana, Bolivia to Kosovo.

1. Instead of needing an optician to test and choose solid lenses with the right shape and thickness, Joshua's glasses have lenses with an empty space inside.

HOLLOW LENSES

2. The wearer injects clear liquid into the space, as much or as little as they need to be able to see clearly.

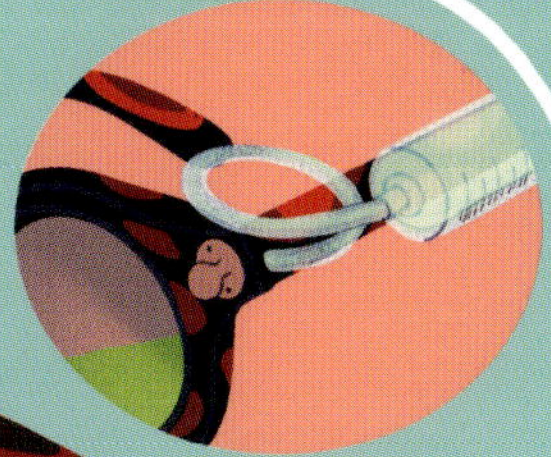

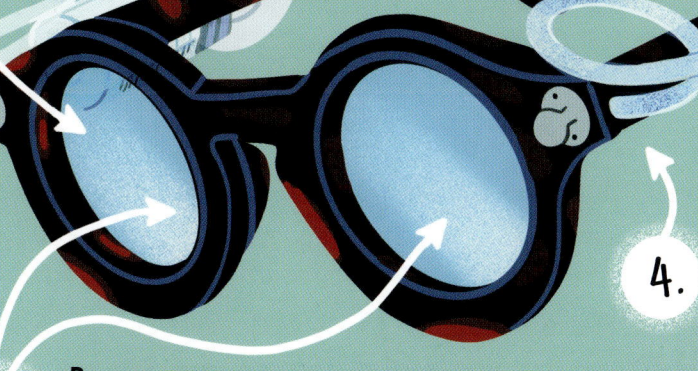

4. The syringes containing the liquid can then be snapped off and the glasses are sealed and ready for wear.

3. By controlling how much liquid fills the space, the wearer decides the curve and thickness of their lenses themselves, within minutes!

MORE LIQUID   LESS LIQUID

GREAT MINDS!

By the age of five, **LOUIS BRAILLE** was entirely blind; he was taught to read using a system for blind people in France, which consisted of touching raised letters on a page. Louis found this to be slow and limiting, and so he devised his own code using raised dots, inspired by military communications. Aged fifteen, he completed his code — which is now called Braille and used all over the world.

From Sushruta in ancient India to Antyllus in ancient Greece, doctors have historically tried to remove cataracts, but these were dangerous, often unsuccessful operations. However, a thousand years ago in Iraq, **AMMAR IBN AL-MAWSILI** successfully removed a cataract with a suction technique, reversing his patient's blindness!

In 1981, **PATRICIA BATH** invented a laser device that makes cataract removal faster and easier. Her tool is now used all over the world, restoring the sight of millions.

RENÉ FAVALORO (1923–2000)
BYPASS SURGERY IN ARGENTINA

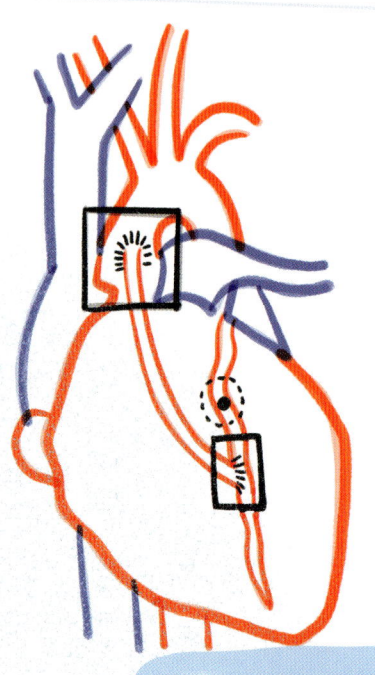

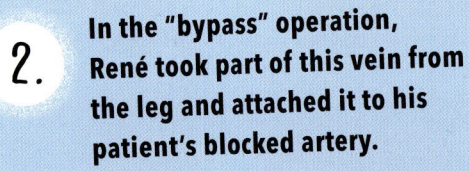

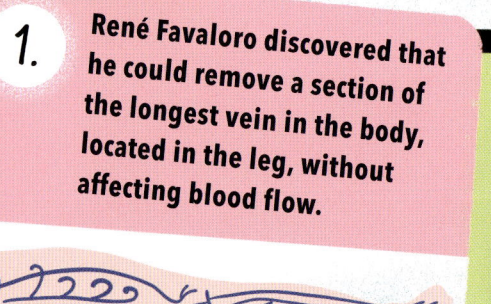

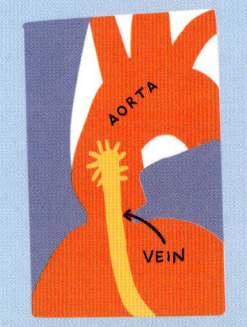

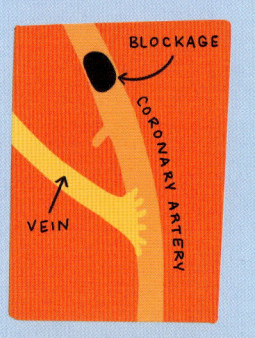

HOW IT WORKS

1. René Favaloro discovered that he could remove a section of the longest vein in the body, located in the leg, without affecting blood flow.

2. In the "bypass" operation, René took part of this vein from the leg and attached it to his patient's blocked artery.

3. By connecting it to the artery on the heart just before and after the blockage, the blood could take a different but clear passage.

AORTA
VEIN
BLOCKAGE
CORONARY ARTERY
VEIN
BLOCKAGE
BYPASS

12

—DID YOU KNOW?—
The "bypass" is one of the most common operations in countries all over the world.

MAKING A DIFFERENCE

Once he had passed his exams to become a doctor, René Favaloro moved from busy Buenos Aires to a small, remote town: "La Pampa". He believed everyone had the right to healthcare whether they were rich or poor, so he built an operating room in La Pampa, trained local people in medicine and set up the first "mobile" blood bank in the area.

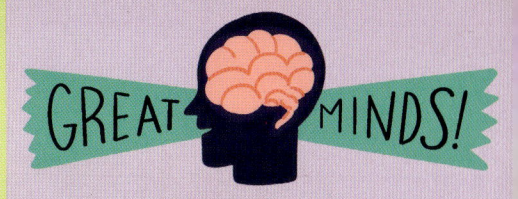

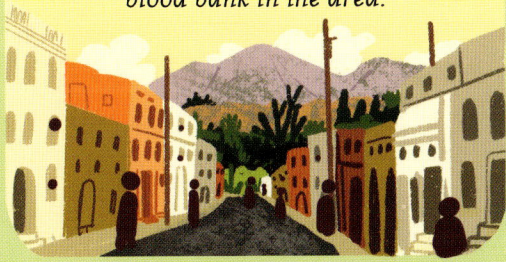

GREAT MINDS!

Thousands of years ago, **NATIVE AMERICAN TRIBES** designed and created medical syringes using bird bones and animal bladders to inject medicines and clean wounds — this technology only reached Europe years later when **ALEXANDER WOOD** used needles to inject medicine in Scotland in the 1800s. Along with surgical tools, Native Americans also discovered special plants that can be used to ease pain, far before modern pain-relief. They brewed American black willow bark to make tea that produces salicylic acid: the main ingredient now used in aspirin!

ABU AL-QASIM AL-ZAHRAWI was a doctor in tenth-century Spain, who wrote an incredibly detailed book on medical science and surgery, ranging from childbirth to infectious diseases. He introduced a collection of over 200 surgical instruments that are now used by surgeons all over the world. He invented surgical scissors, special hooks, forceps, bone saws and much more that made many operations possible and successful.

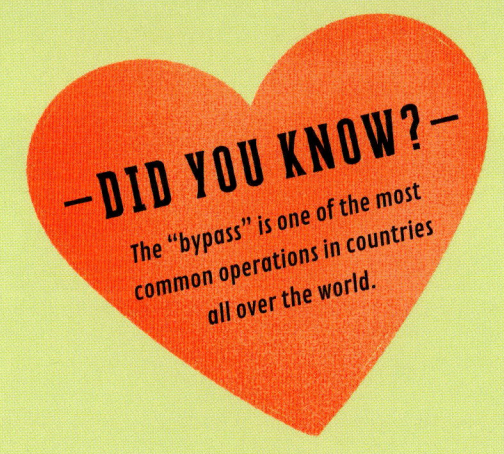

After becoming a doctor, René Favaloro became more and more fascinated by the human heart, and how to operate on it. His interest grew, and he decided to specialize in the study and treatment of hearts. Every day when he finished work, René spent hours studying images to try and better understand the heart and its systems, marvelling at this delicate organ that pumps away to keep us all alive.

A common heart disease blocks the main tubes, or "arteries", that carry blood through the body. If a coronary artery ends up blocked, the person will have a heart attack – which can be deadly. René wondered if there was a way to allow blood to pass by the blocked artery, instead of building up in one place, leading to a heart attack.

His idea was essentially to re-route blood around the problem. In 1967, René carried out this very operation on one of his patients for the first time, and it was a huge success! His creative, clever solution – now called a "bypass" – has saved lives all over the world.

MARITA CHENG
THE TELEPORT ROBOT IN AUSTRALIA

Marita Cheng loved solving problems at school in science and maths, and was intrigued by the idea of robots – so she went on to study Engineering.

She wanted to use her skills to make a difference, and began to think hard about access, and how people who can't move easily can miss out on things many of us take for granted... For example, children who are in hospital for long periods of time, or people with disabilities which mean they can't leave their homes.

Marita wanted to use robotics to allow people to be in "two places at once", which is how she came to design a robot called Teleport. With a Teleport robot, children in hospital can still attend lessons and be with their friends at lunchtime; meanwhile, people with disabilities affecting their movement can use the robot to go to work and meet up with friends.

— BRAIN POWERED! —
Marita has since designed software that means people who are paralysed can control their robot with their brain and eyes, allowing people who aren't able to move their bodies to explore museums, parks and even other countries.

MOVING PARTS
Marita is also creating parts to allow the robot to open doors or pick up food, and hopes all her inventions will help to make people's lives better.

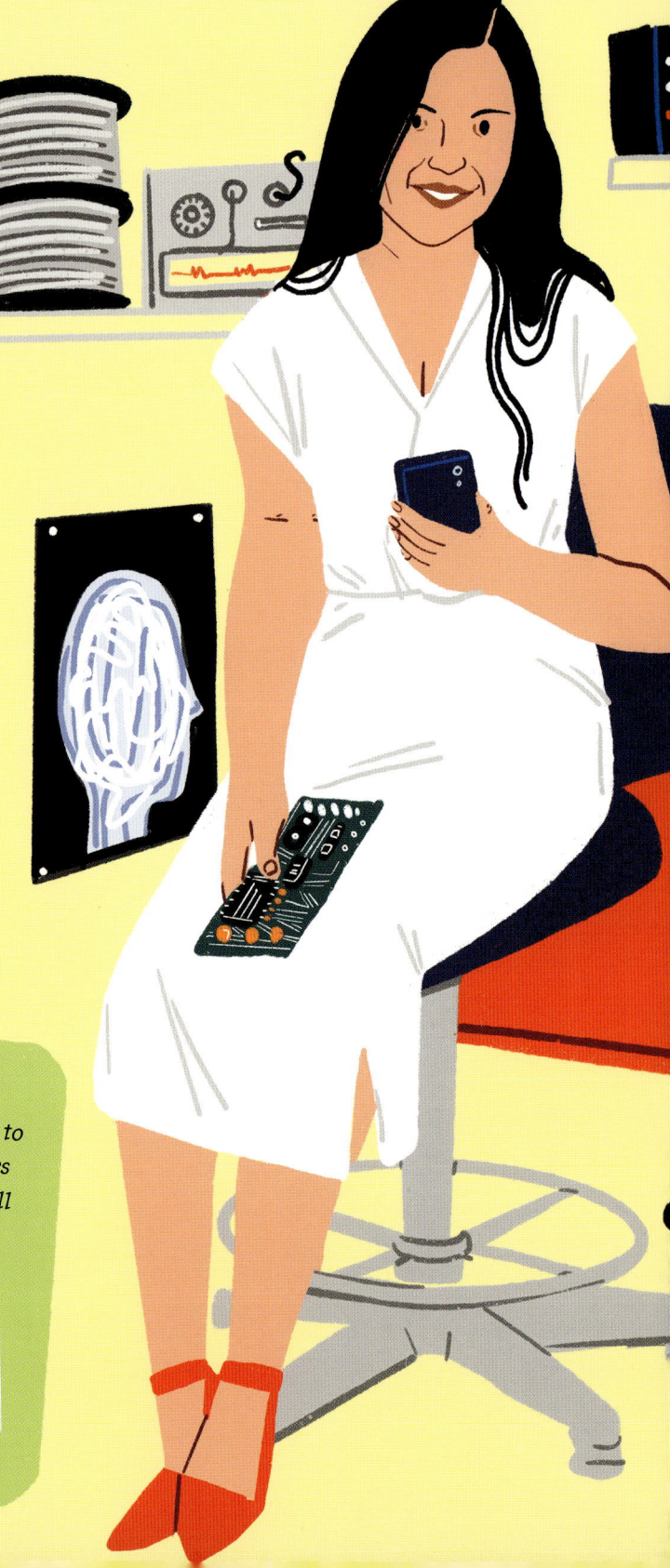

HOW IT WORKS

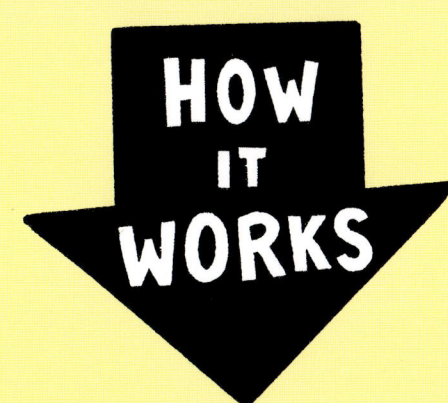

1. The robot can be controlled by phone or computer, and can pick up signals over very long distances.

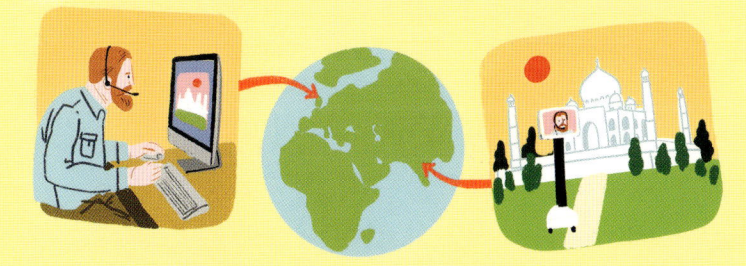

2. For example, you could use it to visit the Amazon jungle while still in your bedroom …

3. navigating the robot around the trees, and making the screen higher or lower to catch a glimpse of a monkey, or to speak to anyone you met on your way!

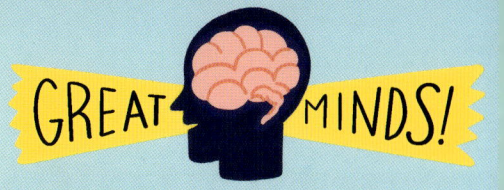

GREAT MINDS!

ISMAIL AL-JAZARI was an inventor and engineer in Turkey in the 1100s, and is known as the "Father of Robotics". Centuries before computers, Al-Jazari invented hundreds of things that have been used by Leonardo Da Vinci, Marita Cheng and many others in this book for their own work. From automatic doors and water clocks, to the first robotics and the sophisticated technology behind engines, you'll see Al-Jazari's work everywhere in your daily life.

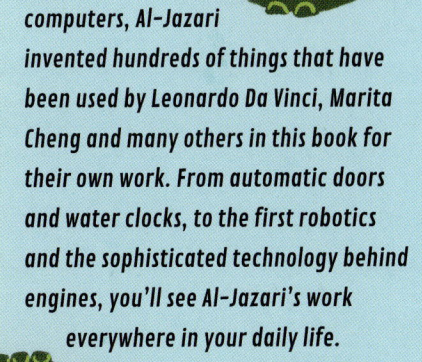

Millions of people around the world struggle to move and walk due to diseases or strokes, and **CONOR WALSH** decided to use robotics to help. He worked with Harvard University to invent a lightweight robotic suit that teaches the body how to work by itself again. His design uses tiny motors, sensors and cables in the cloth, along with clever software, to gently guide the wearer's arms and legs back to work.

KEVIN KUMALA
BIODEGRADABLE PLASTIC IN BALI

HOW IT WORKS

I AM NOT PLASTIC

1. Cassava starch is cheap and easy to find in Indonesia, which makes it the perfect replacement for plastic bags.

2. Unlike normal bags that stick around for hundreds of years causing harm, Kevin's cassava bags will dissolve in water ...

3. and because they're natural, they're actually safe for humans and animals to drink!

–DID YOU KNOW?–

Much of the 340 billion kg of plastic produced per year ends up polluting our planet, in oceans and landfill sites.

MAKING A DIFFERENCE

Since 2016, over 6 million kg of harmful plastic has been replaced with Avani's materials. Kevin believes if everyone replaces their plastics, we can restore our oceans and planet.

Aged eleven, Kevin Kumala went diving for the first time in Bali – he could see for 40 metres underwater, and was captivated by the colourful fish and corals. But when he returned to these waters as an adult, he was horrified at the changes in the ocean: everywhere he looked, there was plastic floating.

From the straws in drinks to the throw-away raincoats motorcyclists wore, from plates to spoons to shopping bags, Kevin suddenly realized that plastic was everywhere. He worked as a biologist and so he started to study "biodegradable" natural materials which could be used instead, without harming the oceans and the planet.

After hours working tirelessly in his lab, he decided to experiment with cassava starch – and found it was a perfect replacement. Not long after, Kevin and his friend started a company called Avani, and have since gone on to produce takeaway boxes, plates and coffee cups from renewable corn starch and sugar cane. After just a few months these turn into compost, which helps feed soil with vitamins!

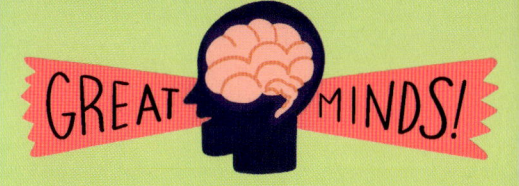

GREAT MINDS!

MIRANDA WANG realized the huge problem of rubbish on a school trip to a waste-processing plant with her best friend **JEANNY YAO**. Miranda and Jeanny worked hard to invent a way to transform previously unrecyclable plastics into useful chemicals. They discovered new methods of breaking down single-use plastics into smaller chemicals which can then be built up again into useful products. They plan to help protect our planet through science.

Indian Chemistry professor **RAJAGOPALAN VASUDEVAN** also set about doing experiments, trying to find positive solutions to the plastic problem. Eventually he discovered he could break down plastics to make roads and pavements! By shredding plastic bags, bottles and packaging, he was able to produce sturdy roads, resistant to weather damage and potholes. Areas in India have already benefitted from his resourceful invention.

17

SARAH TOUMI
ACACIAS FOR ALL IN TUNISIA

Sarah Toumi spent much of her childhood playing in her grandparents' village in Tunisia, where the land was lush and green. As Sarah got older, the effects of modern farming, climate change and a huge lack of rainfall carried the Sahara Desert into their village. The sands that blew in on strong winds were causing crops to fail, and driving people out of their homes.

Sarah began to research and discovered that the acacia tree grows well in dry conditions. Sarah spoke about her findings with local women, who were struggling because of the changing climate, and they were all keen to help – so, together, they began planting acacia trees to form a protective border around their crops.

The results were amazing; delighted, Sarah decided to found "Acacias for All". Alongside planting acacia trees, this organization trains farmers in techniques to help restore the soil, and helps them to sell their crops for a fair price.

AMAZING RESULTS
The results of the acacia tree borders were a triple increase in crop production, healthier soil, preserved water supply and the return of the natural diversity to the area. Sarah has done more than just hold back the desert!

HOW IT WORKS

1. The mighty acacia tree's roots reach 100 metres into the ground to find water.

2. They have special "satellite" roots that spread out to share underground resources with neighbouring trees!

3. As they grow, the acacias form a dense barrier. This prevents the winds from blowing sand onto the villagers' farmland …

4. while also providing gum arabic, which farmers can sell.

TIME TO ACT

By 2030, the beautiful Tunisia Sarah loved was set to be a desert – which drove her to act fast.

MAKING A DIFFERENCE

All the money made from the initiatives is channelled back into the community, and Sarah's dream is for all of North Africa to benefit from these techniques.

GREAT MINDS!

GEORGE WASHINGTON CARVER was born into slavery in the USA, but gained freedom when it was abolished. He had a thirst for knowledge and defied the odds, which were still stacked against Black Americans, to become a brilliant plant expert. He went on to teach poor farmers how to rotate crops throughout the year, which evened out their supply of food as well as their income, and also protected their soil and land in the long run.

YACOUBA SAWADOGO's community's once green farmland in Burkina Faso was quickly turning to desert, and lack of rainfall and failed crops brought desperate hunger to the area. Yacouba worked tirelessly to bring back an ancient African practice called Zaï and managed to plant a forest on barren land. People couldn't understand how he had worked this miracle – in fact, some called him a "madman" and set fire to his forest. But Yacouba never gave up. Over time, the community supported him, and he has since regenerated thousands of hectares of barren land into forest, saving lives and helping our planet.

REEM AL MARZOUQI
FOOT-CONTROLLED CAR IN THE UAE

Reem Al Marzouqi was studying Engineering at university in the UAE, when she saw a video of Jessica Cox – the first person with no arms to become a licensed pilot. She was inspired by Jessica's conviction, as well as the skill with which she flew planes using only her feet.

After learning that despite being able to fly a plane, Jessica could not drive a car, Reem began to think about what she could do to help. At first she tried to adapt existing car designs, but nothing worked… And so, she figured she would have to build a new car from scratch instead.

Her mum supported and encouraged Reem in her work – and it took five attempts over several years before she finally succeeded. Her system is the first of its kind, and with it, anyone born without arms like Jessica, and anyone who has upper body disabilities or paralysis, can drive.

DRIVING CHANGE!
Ever since Reem was young, she has loved understanding how things work, and has always wanted to invent things that help people around her.

— BREAKING BARRIERS —
Reem was the first in her country to gain foreign "patents" for her invention, which means she can make her invention available elsewhere in the world.

HOW IT WORKS

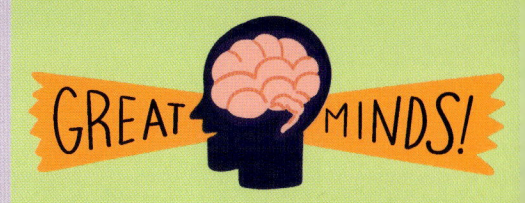

1. In Reem's clever design, there is no steering wheel!

2. Instead, drivers use three foot-controlled pedals on the floor of the car.

3. Each pedal does a separate job, including all of the steering, acceleration and braking functions.

GREAT MINDS!

In East Africa, approximately one in every 200 people needs to use a wheelchair, but can't access or afford a suitable one. While growing up in rural Kenya, **JANNA DEEBLE** met a man named Letu, whose experience of a disease called polio had left him unable to walk. Letu had never been given access to doctors or a wheelchair, and had to slowly crawl anywhere he wanted to go. When Janna was at university, he had an accident that left him unable to walk for weeks. He found he couldn't stop thinking about Letu — and became determined to help. Janna went on to design a new kind of wheelchair called the SafariSeat: perfect for rough or sandy ground, Janna's wheelchair is made from recycled bike parts, and can be built or repaired easily. Adjustable and strong, the SafariSeat gives people like Letu the power of movement and independence.

SONAM WANGCHUK
THE ICE STUPA IN LADAKH, INDIA

KEY WORD: IRRIGATION

Supplying water to land for crops, soil and other uses is called irrigation. Water is essential to human, animal and plant life.

HOW IT WORKS

1. A long pipe carries water from a lake or stream downslope to the villages.

2. By the time water reaches the other end, gravity makes it shoot out powerfully.

Sonam Wangchuk is an engineer who lives in the desert region of Ladakh, high in the Himalayan mountains. Because of climate change, the huge glaciers that once provided villagers with meltwater are now shrinking, leaving people without water for drinking and crops.

Sonam knew that the water shortages happened in summer when rain was in short supply, while in winter there was plenty of unused water. And so, he came up with the idea of an artificial glacier – called an ice stupa.

Over weeks, the constant sprinkle from high up the mountains creates another mountain of ice for the Ladakhi villagers. The grand stupas remain frozen through winter and begin to melt in spring, providing a precious water supply in summer when people and animals are thirsty, and land is dry.

When Sonam trialled his first, 20-metre high stupa, villagers helped to plant thousands of trees, which would be watered by the stupa meltwater – transforming the cold desert into green land. In this way, Sonam's invention protects water, crops, a culture and way of life for Himalayan communities.

–DID YOU KNOW?–
The first ever methods of irrigation were invented in ancient Egypt and Mesopotamia around 6000 BCE, enabling their civilizations to flourish.

3. The air, which is minus 20°C, freezes the water as it falls – creating the stupa.

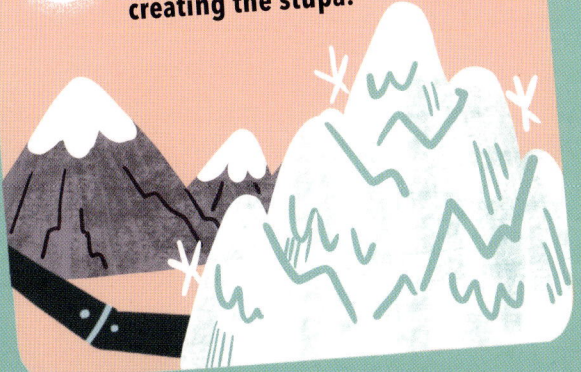

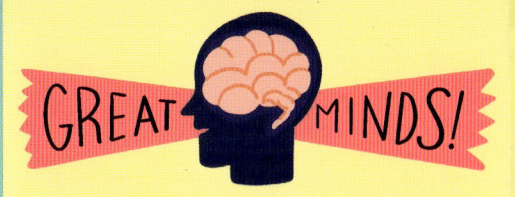

4. In spring the stupa melts, providing villagers with water.

GREAT MINDS!

During World War II, GORDON SATO was imprisoned in America, just for being of Japanese descent. Years later he visited the country of Eritrea, hit hard by war and drought, and his trip sparked memories of his own suffering. Not much grew in the harsh desert and rain was scarce, but Eritrea borders the sea. Gordon studied the only type of tree that can grow in saltwater: the mangrove. He tirelessly researched how he could plant mangroves, and designed the perfect system. In 2001, he planted 40,000 mangrove trees on the coast. Gordon's trees grew and the nearby communities were able to provide themselves with much-needed income and food. In the absence of rain, Gordon turned to the sea instead to bring life, and with his determination to do good, he succeeded.

TEMPLE GRANDIN
THE HUG MACHINE IN AMERICA

When Temple Grandin was growing up, she realized she could "think in pictures". Temple is autistic, and autism wasn't widely understood when she was a child. Loud noises and bright lights would overwhelm her, particularly when she went to school; to reassure herself, she would run to the swings and twist round and round, until she was wrapped up and felt calm again. Temple, like a number of other people on the autistic spectrum, found hugs uncomfortable and difficult, but being squeezed made her feel safe and peaceful.

When she was eighteen, Temple was at her aunt's ranch and saw how the cattle calmed down when they were in a narrow metal corridor, or "chute", which had the effect of squeezing them. It was here that inspiration struck. By then, Temple had engineered many things, from model rockets to cat flaps ... but could she build a hug?

Temple got to work, taking inspiration from that chute to invent her own Hug Machine! She hopped inside and, as the soft sides pressed her, she felt better at once.

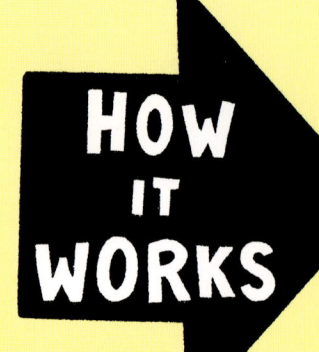

HOW IT WORKS →

MAKING A DIFFERENCE

Temple's Hug Machine is now used as part of several therapy programmes for autistic people in America. She has also developed machines to help improve the comfort and treatment of farm animals.

1. Temple used the same sort of design as the cattle chute, setting up a lever that the user pulls.

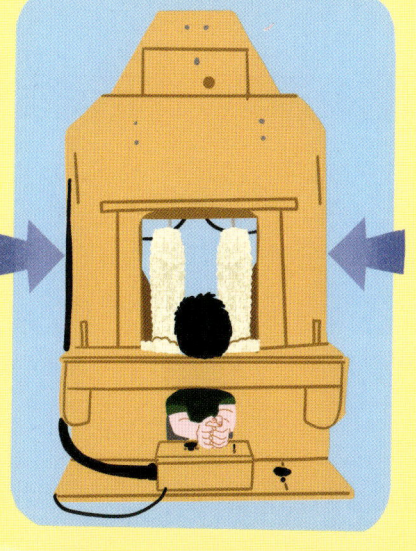

2. When the lever moves, an air cylinder squeezes the side boards closer together.

3. The user sits or lies down between the boards, which are coated in soft cushions, and is given a big comforting "hug" ... without any of the stress and discomfort that may come from hugging a person.

— STARTING SMALL —
When Temple Grandin was young, she loved making paper kites, setting up obstacle courses for her pet dog and building all sorts of things.

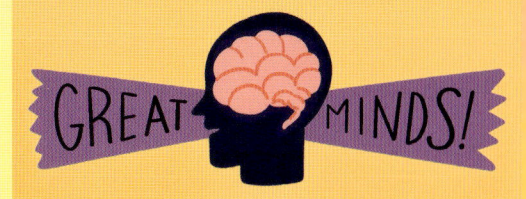

GREAT MINDS!

70 million people use sign languages, but there are over 126 different languages around the world. **JUNTO OHKI** invented the first online sign database to help bridge the gap between languages. It uses a special keyboard to help deaf people easily look up words that correspond to signs in other languages – as well as enter new ones. Thousands use the database in his home country, Japan, and he hopes to expand across the world.

In India, children were often brought to see doctors because they hadn't started talking, only for their families to later discover they were deaf or hard of hearing. If detected early enough, these children could be treated if desired. **NEETI KAILAS** invented a portable device that fits over a newborn baby's head and measures the brain's response to sounds. Her invention quickly and simply diagnoses hearing loss at the earliest possible stage.

25

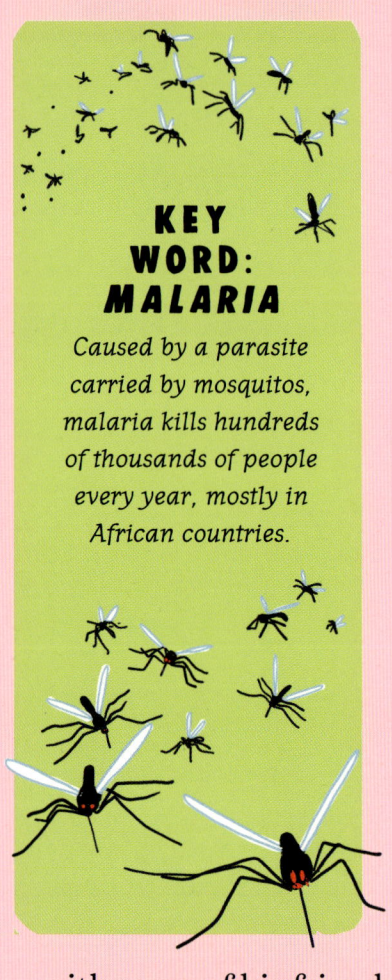

BRIAN GITTA
THE MALARIA TESTING DEVICE IN UGANDA

KEY WORD: MALARIA

Caused by a parasite carried by mosquitos, malaria kills hundreds of thousands of people every year, mostly in African countries.

Like most of his friends, Brian Gitta suffered from a disease called malaria almost every year of his life. Malaria is treatable, but only if it is diagnosed in time – people must make their way to a clinic to be tested, sometimes walking for miles before queuing for hours. A blood sample is taken using a needle, and then long periods pass before the results come back from the lab to confirm malaria. During this wait, people often die.

Brian was a computer scientist, and he wanted to use technology to help people affected by malaria – and to take their pain away quickly. Working together with some of his friends, Brian discovered that if someone is infected, their blood cells change, and tiny magnetic crystal structures appear in their blood.

They invented a testing device that uses light and magnets to check for these crystals, and to see if blood cells have changed. It should even detect malaria in its earliest stages ... making it a very powerful force for good!

NEGATIVE

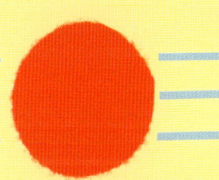

POSITIVE

—PLANNING AHEAD—
Brian's team worked hard to make their testing device portable and affordable, and hope it will benefit people all over Uganda and beyond.

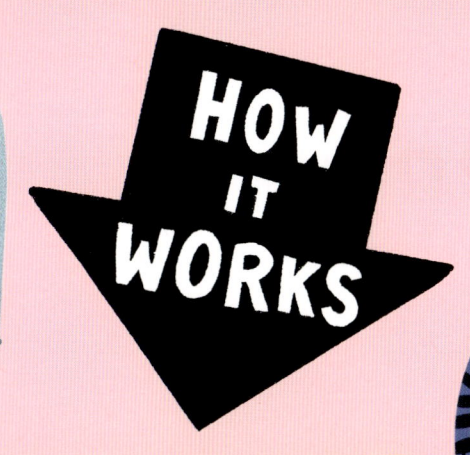

HOW IT WORKS

1. Brian's device uses light and magnets to look through the skin.

2. There is no need for needles, the patient simply puts a clean finger into the testing device to be scanned.

3. Within minutes the results show up, so patients don't need to wait hours or days to find out if they have malaria.

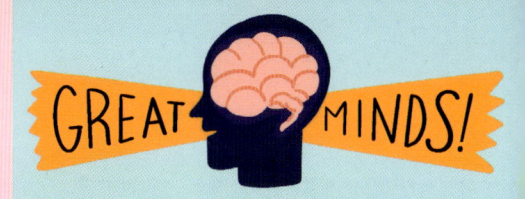

GREAT MINDS!

A "centrifuge" is a piece of equipment that spins liquid samples at high speeds in order to separate out the different things they contain. They can detect many diseases, including malaria and tuberculosis, but are expensive, difficult to transport and require electricity to run. Indian scientist **MANU PRAKASH** was desperate to find another way to diagnose disease cheaply and effectively.

Inspired by a whirligig toy, Manu began playing around with a button threaded on some string, spinning it as fast as it would go — and was amazed at the speed it reached.

He then designed a simple device out of around 15 pence worth of paper, string and plastic, which can spin as fast as an electric centrifuge! Successful at separating liquids and diagnosing diseases, Manu's invention is ideal for poor areas without electricity.

Manu also invented an ingenious 40 pence microscope that can be assembled in minutes. It folds up from being flat like simple origami, and allows the user to see tiny things like blood cells and bacteria.

ABEER SEIKALY
THE COLLAPSIBLE TENT IN JORDAN

KEY PHRASE: SOLAR POWER
If something is solar-powered, it means it can turn energy from the sun into useful electricity.

HOW IT WORKS

1. Made from lightweight but strong fabric, the tent can collapse down to be carried where needed, or expanded to create a shelter.

   UNSTRETCHED STRETCHED

2. The outside fabric is solar-powered, while the inside has large pockets for storage.

3. A clever system for water-collection, and a tank at the top of the tent, allow for showers – and the tent is protected from flooding by drainage.

4. The expandable and shrinkable design means the tent can be opened and ventilated in the heat, and kept closed and cosy in the cold.

28

In Abeer Seikaly's home country of Jordan, there are huge refugee camps where thousands of people who have had to flee their homes because of war now live. Abeer was shocked by the conditions which these refugees were forced to endure: cramped in uncomfortable tents without water, electricity or basic essentials.

Abeer began thinking about how a good shelter means more than just a sheet of material over your head – how it should be dignified. She used her experience as an architect to note all the things the refugees were lacking in the camp, and spent years designing a solution ... the ingenious collapsible tent!

Abeer hopes her tents will provide safe spaces for people who have lost everything – so that they can start to weave a home for themselves again.

WORKING TOGETHER

Abeer involved the communities themselves in the design of the tents, valuing their input and feelings, and wants the tents to be made from locally sourced materials.

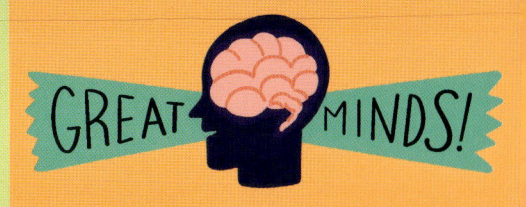

GREAT MINDS!

PRASOON KUMAR designed a clever tent, suitable for all seasons and weathers, for homeless people everywhere. His design fits a family of five, can be assembled and repaired easily, and is perfect for use in cities as well as in the countryside. Since 2013, his company has given shelter to over 4,000 people in desperate need in India, Bangladesh, Cambodia and Nepal.

When **INGRID VACA DIEZ** visited a school in Bolivia, one child told her all they wanted was a house with more space that didn't leak. Ingrid was inspired to use the plastic bottles, which litter spaces all over the world, to build affordable houses. Since then, she has built hundreds of families new homes.

YAHAYA AHMED brought this technology to Nigeria, where it gives young unemployed people important work while providing much-needed sturdy, lasting homes. Once filled with dirt, bottles can be used like bricks, but have the advantage of being much cheaper and reducing plastic waste.

EMMA CAMP
CORAL NURSERIES IN AUSTRALIA

Emma Camp's first glimpse of coral was aged seven in the Bahamas. She couldn't believe the beauty of the reef she saw below: darting fish and swaying corals in every colour and shape created an underwater city! She has been captivated by the ocean ever since, and with corals in particular.

Coral reefs are in trouble: the temperature of the seas is rising thanks to climate change, which can bleach corals and destroy entire reefs in days. When she learnt that more than half of the world's corals have died in the last 30 years, Emma set out to help. She began searching for species of coral that can survive in warmer water, and was surprised to find coral in warm, acidic mangrove lagoons … where she had thought it would be far too difficult for any species to survive.

This new species was more resilient and tougher than most – and with it, Emma had found a glimmer of hope. She and her team used these corals to set up 50 coral "nurseries", which would help more to grow; if ocean temperatures continue to rise, the tougher species being grown in Emma's nurseries may hold the key to saving coral in the future.

TIME TO ACT
Unless we act fast, coral reefs are estimated to completely disappear by 2100, when the sea will be far too warm and acidic.

2022   2100

— DID YOU KNOW? —
Coral reefs are known as the "rainforests of the ocean", as they are unimaginably diverse – home to a quarter of all sea life.

SUPER CORAL!
As well as being home to sea life, reefs filter out pollution and protect coasts against extreme weather like hurricanes.

HOW IT WORKS

1. Emma and her team took "clippings" of the super-survivor mangrove coral to reefs affected by rising sea temperatures.

2. They set up 50 coral nurseries, using a sort of mesh fence with cuttings of different types of coral fixed to it, weighed down close to the sea floor.

3. They planted over 16,000 corals and allowed them to spread across struggling reefs.

4. Emma and her team have also been studying the mangrove corals carefully, to find out what makes them so strong.

GREAT MINDS!

Having seen rubbish harming life in the oceans, **PETE CEGLINSKI** and **ANDREW TURTON** decided that, just like we have bins on land, we also need bins at sea. Together, the pair designed and produced a floating rubbish bin: the container sucks water through a bag that catches and collects different sizes of plastics, as well as other floating debris. These "Seabins" catch around 1500 kg of rubbish every year, making the sea a safer, healthier place.

Seagrass is exactly what it sounds like ... grass under the sea! These underwater fields capture huge amounts of carbon, and provide homes and food for fish, turtles, seahorses and more. Sadly the UK has lost over 90% of its precious seagrass populations, but volunteers of all ages and backgrounds came together with the **WWF, SKY OCEAN RESCUE** and **SWANSEA UNIVERSITY** to grow and plant 1 million seagrass seeds, in the hope that the return of this powerful plant will work wonders for the planet.

SARA SAEED
TELEMEDICINE IN PAKISTAN

Sara Saeed passed her exams to become a doctor in Pakistan; however, she had to stop work after she had her first child. Sara was frustrated: many Pakistani people lived miles and miles away from a healthcare centre, or else were unable to afford the cost. Meanwhile, after the many years she had spent studying to become a doctor, childcare difficulties and family duties meant that Sara, and thousands of female Pakistani doctors like her, had to stay at home.

But then Sara came across "telemedicine", a way of using the internet to link doctors up with people living in poor and rural areas. Sara realized that she could use this to connect home-bound doctors with the people most in need of healthcare – and, with the help of a friend, she set about creating a new online system.

Sara and her friend have already enabled hundreds of female doctors to go back to work, and provided thousands of people with precious access to them. Her ambitious vision for the system is for every doctor to be able to work from home, and for every person to have access to quality healthcare.

– DID YOU KNOW? –
Over half of the people in Pakistan aren't able to access a doctor in person if they fall sick – which makes Sara's creative use of technology a much-needed and powerful tool.

HOW IT WORKS

1. Sara set up E-clinics, where patients from villages and poor areas can visit a nurse near by.

2. The nurse uses an iPad or laptop to video call a doctor.

MAKING A DIFFERENCE

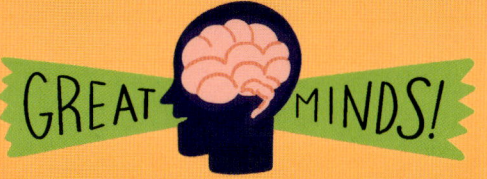

One of Sara's online appointments costs only a very small amount, allowing even very poor families to access healthcare when needed.

3. The doctor can work from the comfort of her own home, seeing the patient through the video call.

4. The doctor can then instruct the local nurse to carry out tests, and dispense medicines when needed.

GREAT MINDS!

Over 1,000 years ago in Saudi Arabia, a nurse named **RUFAIDA AL-ASLAMIA** used her expertise — and kindness — to develop the first ever "mobile" medical care units. She was interested in preventing the spread of disease and made sure that her units were designed to ensure good hygiene. Rufaida worked hard to train other nurses and share her skills, saving many lives in the process. Her idea lives on today, used around the world in warzones and after natural disasters like earthquakes.

200 years ago, **FLORENCE NIGHTINGALE** worked as a nurse and was sent to treat soldiers injured in the Crimean War. When she arrived at the hospital with her team, she was horrified to see it overcrowded and dirty, with rats running around. Her team cleaned the place from top to bottom; before long, far fewer men were dying of diseases. Florence realized the power of hygiene and made cleanliness a top priority in hospital care.

GLORIA ASARE
BAMBOO CHARCOAL IN GHANA

TIME TO ACT
As more rainforest is destroyed each year, animals, plants and Indigenous peoples become threatened.

MAKING A DIFFERENCE
By working to introduce bamboo fuel to struggling communities, Gloria broke the cycle of poverty and climate change. Fewer people died from smoke inhalation, and the soil and water in the ground was protected.

EMPOWERING!
Gloria also empowers thousands of women in creating bamboo products to sell, giving them precious income.

Gloria Asare saw green land in Ghana dry up into barren desert because of climate change, which meant local farmers could no longer earn a living.

This forced people to find other ways to make money: ancient timber forests were being burnt to the ground in order to create charcoal, which people would sell as fuel... But burning wood charcoal gives off harmful fumes, and by destroying the trees, people were contributing towards global warming.

Gloria had been to visit China, where she saw Chinese bamboo farms and realized tropical bamboo grass, which grows naturally in Ghana, could be the answer to this problem – as a better, cleaner source of fuel than charcoal.

Gloria set up an organization to grow and harvest bamboo in Ghana, focusing on helping those most in need. Now, she educates communities on climate change and empowers them to use bamboo, rather than timber, for their fuel.

HOW IT WORKS

1. Bamboo grows many times faster than timber.

2. The entire plant, including the stem and branch, can be used to make charcoal fuel!

3. Even a small amount of bamboo produces a very large amount of heat and it burns without smoke, preventing lung damage.

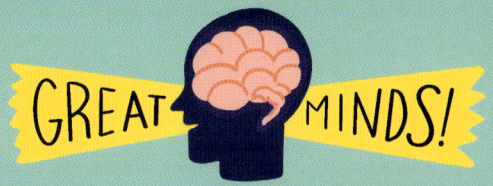

GREAT MINDS!

During an energy crisis in the Philippines, **ALEXIS BELONIO** invented a stove that burns one of Asia's most common waste products: rice husks. People had burnt rice husks before, but it was expensive and produced unhealthy soot. Alexis' new design burns cleanly and safely, while being affordable and giving out half as much harmful carbon as other fuels. Instead of selling his invention, he gives his designs away for free.

The Indigenous **MATSÉS PEOPLE** from the Amazon jungle in Peru and Brazil have a far-reaching knowledge of the healing properties of plants. Some of the tribe's most skilful healers were dying of old age, and their expertise was dying with them, so the tribe decided to act: they compiled a 1,000-page encyclopaedia in their native language, documenting the uses of thousands of plants – from treating snake bites to stomach diseases. By recording these secrets, precious culture as well as important information was preserved.

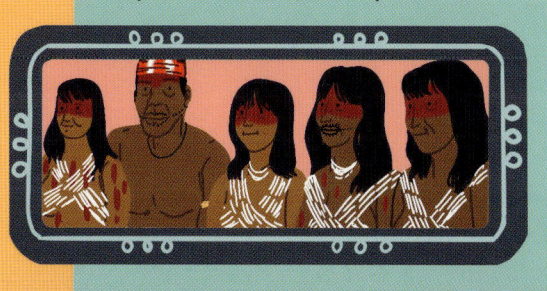

WILHELM RÖNTGEN (1845–1923)
X-RAYS IN GERMANY

At the time Wilhelm Röntgen was working as a scientist, doctors had no way to see inside the body of someone if they got hurt or ill – they'd just have to guess what, and where, the problem was.

One day, Wilhelm was doing an experiment in his lab when something unexpected happened. He was exploring "fluorescence", which is when things glow or give off light. He filled a tube with a special material that glowed when electricity passed through it, and was shocked when he noticed that a screen across the room had begun to glow too. The screen had been coated in the same special material he had put inside the tube, and Wilhelm realized that the tube was sending out an invisible stream of rays.

Wilhelm had discovered a new form of radiation by accident. He named the mystery rays "X-rays", with the "X" meaning "I don't know"; this lucky discovery went on to transform medicine for the better, helping doctors diagnose and treat problems inside the body without the need for guesswork.

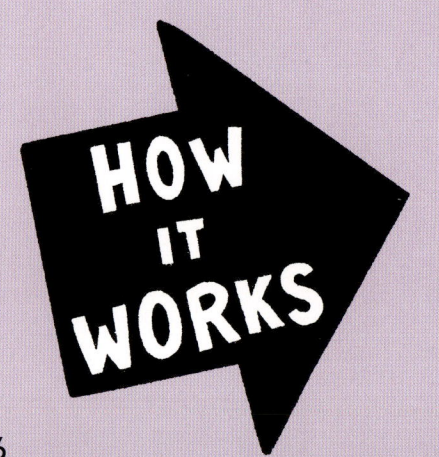

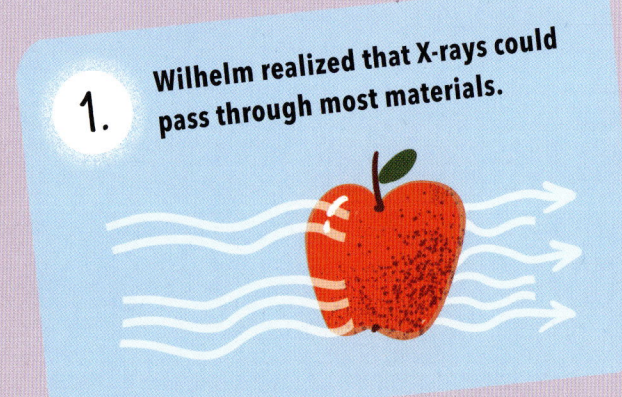

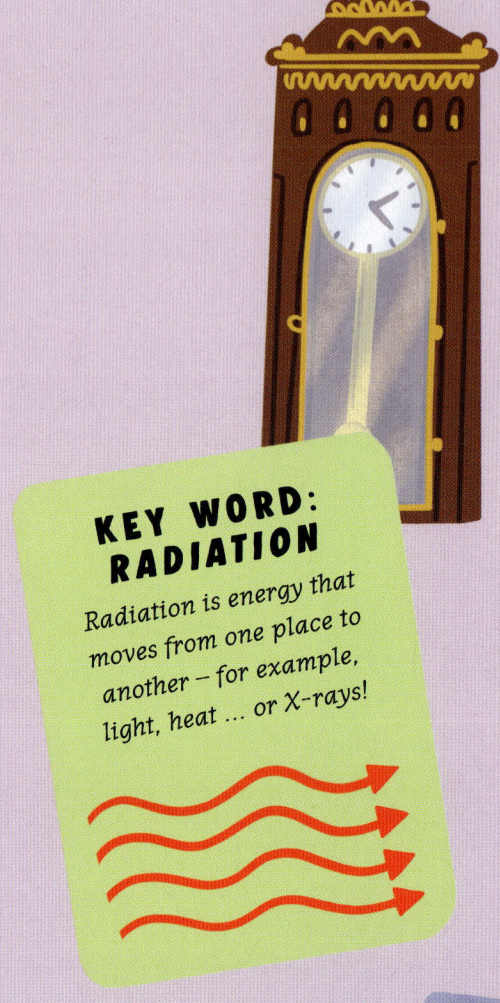

KEY WORD: RADIATION

Radiation is energy that moves from one place to another – for example, light, heat ... or X-rays!

HOW IT WORKS

1. Wilhelm realized that X-rays could pass through most materials.

2. X-rays cast shadows of solid objects on to film. A bit like when you play shadow puppets, projecting shapes on to a wall, X-rays cast black and white images of what they pass through.

MAKING A DIFFERENCE

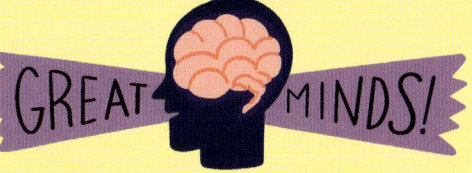

This powerful tool is used in hospitals all over the world every day, and has saved many lives.

3. Wilhelm took the first ever X-ray image of his wife's hand!

4. X-rays travel easily through muscle, less easily through bone and not at all through metal, so his wife's bones and wedding ring showed clearly in the first X-ray image.

GREAT MINDS!

The scientist **MARIE CURIE** developed Wilhelm Roentgen's X-ray machine further, designing a smaller, portable X-ray unit. Her invention was invaluable in World War I, saving the lives of many injured soldiers. Today she's best remembered for her important research into radioactivity with her husband; together, they discovered radioactive elements found in nature which are now safely used to treat cancer patients. Marie was also the first person ever to receive two Nobel Prizes for her work!

IBN AL-HAYTHAM was an Iraqi scientist who lived in the eleventh century. He was unfairly imprisoned by the king of Egypt, and it was during this time that he came to understand how we see objects. He realized that light rays travel in straight lines — and when they bounce off objects and enter our eyes, they form an image. This helped him to invent the "camera obscura", or "pinhole camera". Using a box with a small hole and three candles, Ibn Al-Haytham laid the groundwork for the invention of modern cameras.

HOW IT WORKS

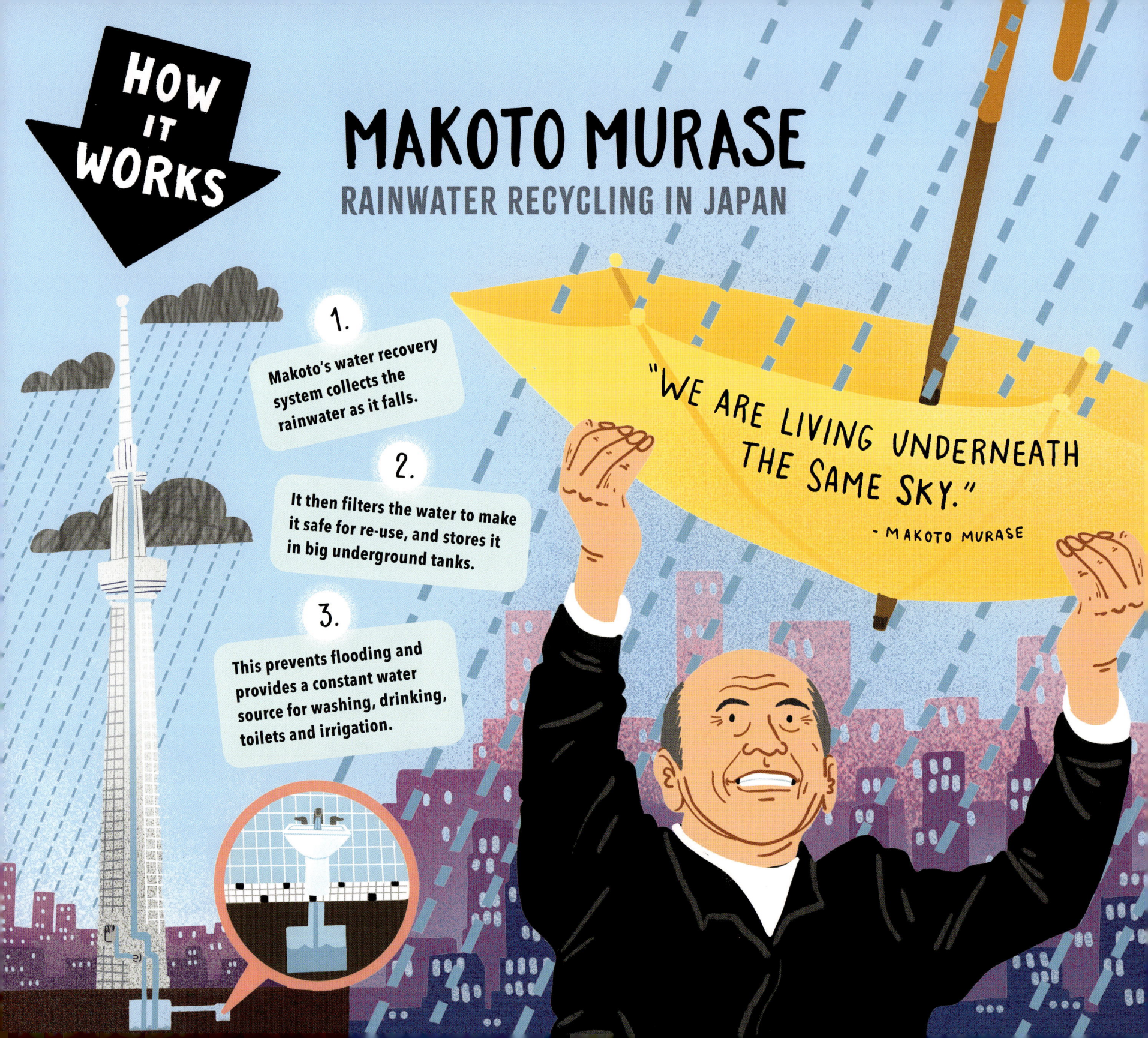

MAKOTO MURASE
RAINWATER RECYCLING IN JAPAN

1. Makoto's water recovery system collects the rainwater as it falls.

2. It then filters the water to make it safe for re-use, and stores it in big underground tanks.

3. This prevents flooding and provides a constant water source for washing, drinking, toilets and irrigation.

"WE ARE LIVING UNDERNEATH THE SAME SKY."
— MAKOTO MURASE

—SKY-WATER—

Makoto is known by the nickname "Dr Skywater", because he calls rainwater "sky-water" like his ancestors did. They saw sky-water as a precious gift from the heavens that should be honoured and respected.

Japan has a rainy season called the "tsuyu" every year, which brings stuffy weather and sudden downpours of rain … and when Makoto Murase was working for the government in Tokyo, his district was badly flooded. Makoto looked around at the damage done to his city and wondered how water, the very thing that gives us life, can also cause such destruction.

This led Makoto to develop a clever way to recycle rainwater: a design that turns rainwater from an annual problem into a useful resource. It was first trialled in the huge Sumo Stadium in Tokyo, and was a great success. Now, all new buildings in Tokyo are required to recycle rainwater, and thousands of existing buildings have adopted the excellent system.

Makoto has since turned his attention to the millions of communities around the world who lack access to fresh water. Some can't afford to pay for clean water, and others don't have a supply near by … but of course, sky-water is free!

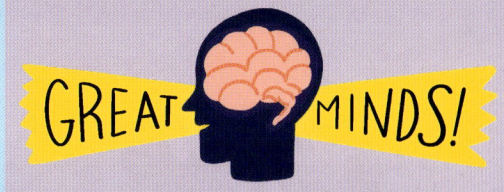

MAKING A DIFFERENCE

Unclean drinking water causes millions of deaths around the world: Makoto is now working to make sure that people from Nepal to Indonesia, and Bangladesh to the Philippines, can benefit.

GREAT MINDS!

PIET HENDRIKSE noticed people from villages near his home in South Africa struggling to carry heavy water containers. He knew how finding clean water was only part of the difficulty; transporting it home often took hours of walking in the heat, leaving people with neck and back injuries. Piet designed a unique doughnut-shaped water container with a rope through its centre, so that it could be pulled along the ground. With Piet's Q-Drum, 50 litres of water can be easily rolled!

MIKKEL VESTERGAARD FRANDSEN was nineteen years old when he saw many people had no choice but to drink dirty water in Nigeria. With the support of his family business, Mikkel created the LifeStraw. His water-filtering design packed into a straw can be used to drink dirty water: as you suck the water towards your mouth, tubes inside the LifeStraw trap disease-causing bacteria and dirt, leaving you with safe, clean water.

TOPHER WHITE
THE TREE PHONE IN INDONESIA

Topher White was working at a gibbon reserve in Indonesia when he heard the unmistakable growl of a chainsaw near by. He ran towards the sound and was horrified to see a majestic old teak tree cut to the ground by a poacher – who ran away when he noticed Topher.

Topher knew that the destruction of forests, or "deforestation", has a terrible effect, from worsening climate change to threatening animals like elephants, orangutans and tigers. The jungle is dense, making it hard to see very far, and Topher realized that the most powerful system to track poachers would rely on sound instead of sight – the rainforest is constantly humming, pulsing and squawking, and every noise holds precious information.

His idea was to attach old smartphones with solar panels to trees, and to record sounds in the surrounding areas. After spending a year on his design, Topher installed the first phone in a tree in Indonesia. He was worried it wouldn't work, but within minutes the new system showed that someone was sawing a tree near by!

GOOD NEWS TRAVELS FAST!

Topher's ingenious tracking systems are already in operation in Indonesia, Brazil and Cameroon.

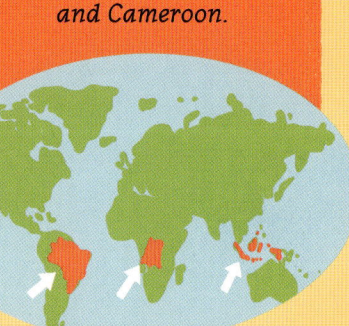

HOW IT WORKS

1. Loggers begin cutting down a tree.
2. Smartphones, which get their power from solar panels, are installed on nearby trees.
3. One of the smartphones picks up the sound of chainsaws, and of logging trucks.
4. The smartphone sends an alert to forest rangers.
5. Forest rangers move quickly, to catch the poachers and protect the area.

GREAT MINDS!

Eye-specialist **DR ANDREW BASTAWROUS** moved from the UK to rural Kenya. Most people didn't have access to any eye care, and some of the villages he visited had no electricity or roads, but he noticed they almost always had phone signal. Andrew wondered if there was a way to use mobile phone technology to test people's eyes, instead of high-tech, heavy and expensive equipment. Together with his team, he invented an eye examination kit to be used on a smartphone. People can be easily trained to use it, and the simple app has the potential to improve eye care for millions of people.

— DID YOU KNOW? —

Half of the world's forests have already been destroyed, and around 40,000 hectares of rainforest are logged each day.

PEARL KENDRICK (1890–1980) & GRACE ELDERING (1900–1988)
THE WHOOPING COUGH VACCINE IN AMERICA

HOW IT WORKS

1. Pearl and Grace asked infected children to cough on circular plates called petri dishes.

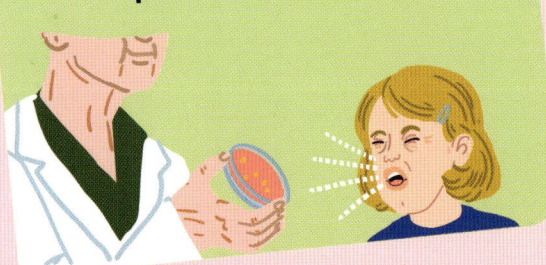

2. Using these samples, Pearl and Grace were able to grow and study the bacteria that caused whooping cough.

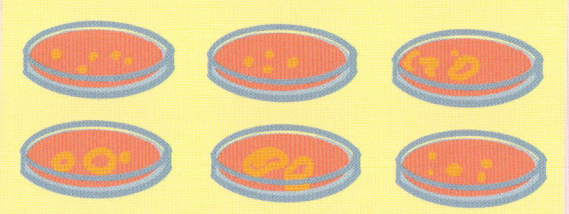

3. Pearl and Grace worked with their whole community to perfect the vaccine; they also tested it by injecting it into themselves!

KEY WORD: VACCINE

A vaccine trains your body to protect itself against a virus or infection before you become ill with it. This is often achieved by injecting you with a weak form of the virus.

– DID YOU KNOW? –

Around 6,000 children used to die in the USA each year from whooping cough – Grace and Pearl's vaccine has saved thousands upon thousands of lives.

GREAT MINDS!

After World War II, **LONEY CLINTON GORDON** began working with Grace and Pearl in their lab. She developed and improved their existing vaccine, testing thousands of bacteria strains. The women then combined vaccines for diphtheria, tetanus and whooping cough into one injection, now used all around the world.

In the early eighteenth century, **LADY MONTAGU** befriended Turkish women during her stay in the Ottoman Empire and learnt about their ancient medical practices, which used an approach similar to modern vaccines. This principle was the basis of Edward Jenner's smallpox vaccine and Louis Pasteur's rabies vaccine, among others.

Almost 1,000 years ago, a Persian scientist named **IBN SINA** came up with the idea of quarantine: isolating people infected with a disease to prevent its spread. 700 years before microscopes, he also described how diseases spread through microbes, and how to protect against them.

In America during the 1930s, Pearl Kendrick and Grace Eldering became friends while working as scientists. Both of them had suffered from the often-deadly whooping cough in their childhoods, and though other scientists had already tried for years to produce vaccines against the disease, none of them worked well.

Pearl and Grace remembered the painful, endless coughing they had suffered, and felt grateful to have survived – so, when the contagious cough began spreading quickly in their neighbourhood, they decided to do something. After a long day's work, Pearl and Grace would feed their dogs, grab some dinner and then set out to visit families with sick children.

The pair met so many parents who were desperate for their children to recover. This spurred them on to work day and night, organizing volunteer nurses, doctors and parents to help – and, after years of tiring work, they finally reached their goal. Grace and Pearl's determination had at last paid off: they had developed a vaccine that would protect children against whooping cough!

4. Pearl and Grace appealed to important figures like First Lady Eleanor Roosevelt, and eventually got the funding to make the vaccine available nationwide.

RICHARD TURERE
THE LION LIGHTS IN KENYA

From the age of nine, Richard Turere looked after his dad's cattle in Kenya. Richard knew that his family's herd, like other Maasai herders', was always at risk from hungry lions – and one morning, he woke to discover his dad's only bull had been killed overnight.

The cows are the Maasai people's source of income, and so farmers would sometimes kill the lions to protect their herds. And while Richard was devastated to lose his family's precious bull, he was also very sad about the lions dying…

Richard hoped there was a way to make peace between the lions and the Maasai. One day after dark, he tried scaring the lions away using fire: to his dismay, this just helped the lions see the cattle they wanted to eat! Next he tried a scarecrow, but the lions simply didn't care.

Richard refused to give up, and one night while he was walking around holding a torch, he realized something. Not a single lion tried to come near the cattle – they were scared of the moving light. The next day, Richard set to work making a flashing device that mimicked human movement with a torch. Just as he'd hoped, the lions finally stayed well away!

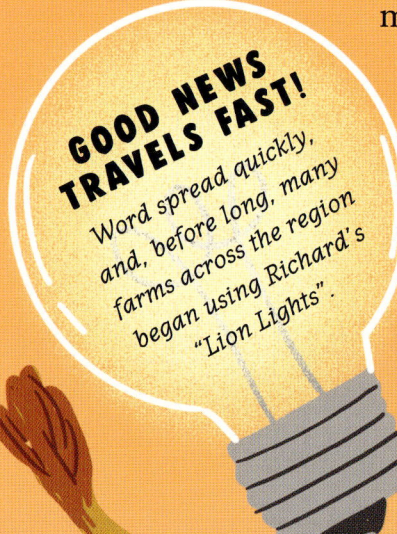

GOOD NEWS TRAVELS FAST!
Word spread quickly, and, before long, many farms across the region began using Richard's "Lion Lights".

MAKING A DIFFERENCE
Richard's cheap, simple machine keeps cattle safe from lions and, as a result, keeps the lions safe from people.

HOW IT WORKS

1. Richard found a solar panel, flashing bulbs, a box with switches and a car battery in rubbish tips.

2. He fitted the flashing bulbs onto poles and placed them around the cattle enclosure. They connected to the box and car battery, which was powered by the solar panel.

3. At night the bulbs flash on and off automatically, to create the effect of a moving torch.

GREAT MINDS!

DR JANE GOODALL loved reading books about animals when she was a child and in 1960 she went to Tanzania to study chimpanzees. Jane taught us more about chimps than anyone had before — she learnt about them as individuals and saw them modify twigs to use as tools! In the UK, children can learn about animals with Jane's schools programme Roots & Shoots (www.rootsnshoots.org.uk).

SINKEY BOONE worked as a fisherman, catching shrimp from the sea floor using a big trawling net. Turtles sometimes got caught by accident, and once they were tangled up they would die. Sinkey invented a device that allows shrimp to be caught while providing an escape route for turtles. His "Turtle Excluder Device" design has been developed further and is now used all over the world by fishermen, saving turtles and also sharks, rays and crabs.

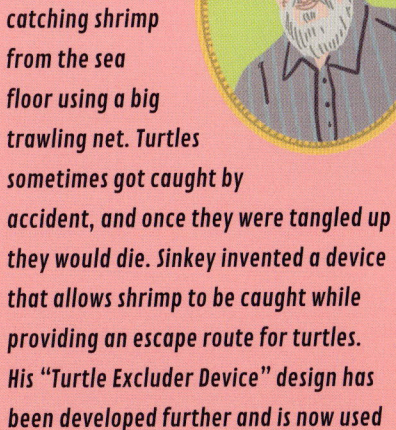

45

NEXT STEPS

What makes all of these inventors so inspiring is their care for the people, animals and planet around them. Our world needs more creative minds and warm hearts, working together to solve the problems we face.

So: you've read this book and have (I hope!) been inspired by the incredible people you've met along the way. Now what?

TOP INVENTOR TIPS:

1. Think outside the box. You can only invent something if you learn to stretch your mind BEYOND what already exists. (Besides, boxes are boring!) Try to see possibilities rather than limits: if you can't see it, maybe you can create it!

2. Find what interests you. It might be related to animals or plants, food, water, health, people, or absolutely anything else. Start identifying problems or gaps in the current situation, and then let your brain cogs whirr and click as you begin imagining solutions.

3. Keep a notebook and pen handy, and jot down any ideas that pop into your mind. Sketching out diagrams and keeping a record of your thoughts during the process can be useful.

4. Always keep the side-effects of your inventions in mind. If something is solving one problem but creating others, it might be worth rethinking. Make sure your ideas are as environmentally friendly as possible.

5. Find a local STEM club or group you can join: you'll meet fellow aspiring inventors and learn new skills that might help you to develop and realize your invention dreams.

6. Remember to keep your mind and heart in gear at all times… Again, truly good ideas involve a bit of both!

7. Never give up. Anyone who has ever invented anything will definitely have had to be persistent, and ready to adapt their ideas and designs to meet new challenges. Often, many, many versions of an invention will be developed before the "final" design is reached – and even then, a really good inventor will carry on thinking about how it can be made even better. You might have a hundred ideas before your ground-breaking, world-changing one comes about. Imagine if you gave up at idea number 99!

8. If you're ever lacking inspiration, why not pick up this book? These inventors are "ordinary" people like you or me – and yet, they're working to change the world in beautiful ways.

FOR EVERY READER OF THIS BOOK, OUR WORLD NEEDS YOUR SPARK
NOW MORE THAN EVER. TREASURE IT AND LET IT LIGHT YOUR WAY.
FOR U, THE COOLEST INVENTOR I KNOW. – H.N.K.

TO MY HUSBAND, MICHAEL – S.P.

First published 2022 by Walker Books Ltd
87 Vauxhall Walk, London SE11 5HJ

2 4 6 8 10 9 7 5 3 1

Text © 2022 Hiba Noor Khan
Illustrations © 2022 Salini Perera

The right of Hiba Noor Khan and Salini Perera to be identified as author and illustrator respectively of this work
has been asserted in accordance with the Copyright, Designs and Patents Act 1988

This book has been typeset in Alice

Printed in Thailand

All rights reserved. No part of this book may be reproduced, transmitted or stored in an information retrieval system in any form or by any means,
graphic, electronic or mechanical, including photocopying, taping and recording, without prior written permission from the publisher.

British Library Cataloguing in Publication Data:
a catalogue record for this book is available from the British Library

ISBN 978-1-4063-9733-8

www.walker.co.uk